THE
BLACK ECONOMIC
EMPOWERMENT
SYSTEM
(BEES)

THE BLACK ECONOMIC EMPOWERMENT SYSTEM (BEES)

HOW TO SYSTEMATICALLY EMPOWER A BLACK COMMUNITY

ANTHONY RICE, JR.

Published by BOOK YOUR LIFE, Publishers
1511M Sycamore Avenue, #121
Hercules, CA 94547 | 888-444-7552
info@bookyourlife.us

Anthony Rice, Jr., CEO
Economic Empowerment Systems, Inc.
19146 Midway Road | Southfield, MI | 48075
(313)505-0700 | aricejr1@msn.com

Library of Congress Cataloging-in-Publication Data available
ISBN: 978-0-692-90694-1
Paperback, First Edition

Printed in the United States
17 16 15 14 13 12 11 9 7 5 3 1

ACKNOWLEDGMENTS

My children – Avery, Anthony lll, Alia & Aaron for inspiring me to take on all challenges; My Parents – Anthony Sr. & Elaine for giving me an abundance of love, support, spiritual guidance and believing in me; My Brother & Sister Derrick & Nicole for supporting me and listening to my ideals all night and for many decades; My extended family and friends for believing in me.

Virginia A. Rice for believing in and supporting my dreams at their embryonic stage; Robert D. Black for being a friend and brother for over 40 years and introducing me to an organization that welcomed BEES; Jeff Green for welcoming and actively implementing BEES into his organization; Pape Ndiaye for welcoming and actively implementing BEES into his business; Joann Anderson for taking the time to enlighten me about the power of having the word Black in front of the words Economic Empowerment System; Donald Steele for taking the time to provide me with spiritual guidance when I was in need; James Clingman and George Fraser for taking the time to provide me with feedback that was inspiring and constructive during the genesis of launching BEES.

My support team – Shamika Stokes (Meks Creations/Graphic Art); Ashish (ICAD Animation/Graphic Art and Video;) Barbara Hatcher (Educator); and Wanda Lee-Stevens (Book Your Life/Publishing Services).

My virtual mentors (people that I've listened to on video for many hours) Claud Anderson and Dick Gregory for teaching me to take my "upside down glasses" off, and put on the "magic glasses". The late Wayne Dyer and Abraham Hicks for helping me understand spirituality and the power of the universe; John A. Powell for helping me understand the "pros" of an inclusive system and the "cons" of an exclusive system; Les Brown, Eric Thomas, Tony Robbins, C. T. Fletcher for helping to motivate me to "get my grind on" and never stop.

CONTENTS

INTRODUCTION

THE BLESSING

It was the early 1990s, and after being laid off, I was working for an accounting temporary employment agency. I needed some supplemental income, however, because I was going to be getting married in a year. Looking in the Want Ads I saw a posting for a Locker Room Attendant. The job appeared interesting because I thought it was probably a supervisory position, and I knew it was at a local health club. I could get paid and also be able to work out for free. In the interview, I found out I could work out for free, but it was not even close to a supervisory position; the duties involved cleaning towels, washing showers, and shining shoes, all within the confined walls of the men's locker room. By that time in my life I had my college degree. I had held positions as a Staff Accountant, Comptroller and Manager of Operations. I had achieved my own office, carried a briefcase to work, and had a sports car. In other words, it was beneath me to accept a job so as a menial Locker Room Attendant.

Then a voice (in my mind it was God/The Universe) said *"Anthony! If you get off your high horse and scrub these floors for me with a toothbrush, I will bless you."* Honestly, the last thing a Black man wants to hear from anyone, least of all God, is to get on the floor and scrub anything! Especially one with a college degree. But in the words of Denzel

Washington, *"Do what you have to do, to do what you want to do."* So I did just that.

As it turns out, it was an exclusive health club with an affluent and wealthy clientele. After working there several months, I started handing my resume to members who I knew were managers and owners of businesses. Shortly after that, I decided to hand one to the owner of the health club, because I knew he also owned a corporate office next to the health club.

By this time, we had seen each other at **5am (3 to 5 days a week),** and I had made sure my customer service skills were at an A+.

As he looked over my resume he said, "I didn't know you had a college degree." Before I knew it, I was hired into his computer company as a Financial Systems Operator. Then I discovered not only did he own the health club and the computer company, but also a software development company and about 13 manufacturing plants across the country. One day while entering my manager's office to discuss some business, I saw a book on his desk called ***Common Cents–The ABC Performance Breakthrough***: *How to Succeed with Activity-Based Costing,* by Peter B.B. Turney. The words "Common Cents" caught my attention, so I asked what the book was about. He said it was a method the company was about to implement in its software package. He asked if I wanted to read it, and as I did, I felt a connection with the book that I had never felt before. I could not read it fast enough.

As I reflect now, the reason I felt such a special connection is because the book was the starting point of the blessing that had been given me. After becoming proficient with the theory of Activity-Based Costing, I was promoted to Corporate

Activity-Based Costing Consultant, where I successfully initiated the implementation of multiple ABC manufacturing projects. Shortly thereafter, however, a corporate "realignment" took place, and I was laid off. So I decided to start my own business in 1993—initially as an ABC Consultant. My first client was an insurance brokerage firm that questioned my ability to implement ABC in their company (at that point in my career I had only performed Activity-Based Costing in the manufacturing industry).

They gave me the opportunity anyway, but with a special request. As an insurance broker in addition to increasing their profitability by reducing cost, they also wanted to increase their income. It was this request that transformed me from an Activity-Based Costing Consultant to a Profit Consultant. And that transformation led to the creation of the Profit Consulting Methodology (PCM). PCM is equivalent to

Activity-Based Costing + Activity-Based Revenue (another innovative approach that I created).

After the evolution of the Profit Consulting Methodology, I found I could successfully improve the performance, profitability, and/or process flow for any project, department, or company I took on, in any field or industry. In addition, PCM provided me with a tool to create self-financing "mini-economies", which came in handy, since I could not get a loan from a bank. I learned that the Profit Consulting Methodology's ultimate power is in teaching you how to clearly define your goal and to look at that goal as a project; and once you have encapsulated that goal into a project, determine the activities (units of work) and resources associated with that goal. Then it teaches you to gather and format data about those activities and resources that relate to the goal, and in a correlating effort, how to display and channel that information back toward the goal.

It has been my experience that when this approach is applied correctly, it will ensure your success on any project. And it was this knowledge base that lead to the genesis of the Economic Empowerment System. One dynamic author and a key influencer of Black economic empowerment, and someone I follow, Dr. Claud Anderson, states, *"...It is not civil rights. It is not integration that'll give you equal rights and equal opportunity. It is what you own and control that makes a difference in your society. If you own and control nothing, you'll get nothing."*

The Evolution of an Intellectual Revolution

In 1995, I attended the Million Man March, and for first time I felt like part of a group, instead of just an individual. One million plus Black men, from all parts of our country, north, south, east and west, showed up in solidarity, taking a stand, and pledged to unite in personal responsibility and family values. Not since the Civil Rights marches and the March on Washington had so many Black men in America come together with this display of brotherhood. I heard words like atonement and economic empowerment, which moved me so much that I started thinking at first consciously, and then subconsciously, about how to create and develop economic empowerment projects. As a matter of fact, I started applying the economic empowerment system to my business, which allowed me to successfully take on projects worth hundreds of thousands, and even some projects worth millions of dollars, without ever receiving a loan from a bank.

But then, in 2013, almost 20 years after hearing that first voice, **I heard it again;** **(God/The Universe) said** ***"Anthony! I did not give that blessing to you to keep for yourself. I gave it to you to share with others."*** To put it more simply: "Each one, teach one," is an African-American proverb born from the denial of education during slavery. With this book, it is my goal to educate and train as many people as possible how to successfully develop, implement, and sustain the BEES. So here we are at the starting point of an intellectual revolution via the Overview of the Black Economic Empowerment System.

The OVERVIEW
of the
BLACK ECONOMIC
EMPOWERMENT SYSTEM (BEES)

PHASE ONE: The Introduction to the BEES

At this level you will learn the history of BEES and be introduced to its basic parts.

PHASE TWO: The Theory and Approach to the BEES

This is where you will learn more about the core nucleus of BEES, which includes 6 (six) parts.

11

PHASE THREE: The Application of the BEES

Here you will learn: 1) The Composition of BEES, 2) How to Assemble/Create BEES and, 3) How to Continuously Improve BEES.

PHASE
ONE

"When you are a successful business person, you are only as good as your team. No one can do every deal alone."

Earvin "Magic" Johnson

THE INTRODUCTION TO THE BEES

Hello and welcome to the Introduction to the Black Economic Empowerment System (BEES).

BEES evolved from the **Economic Empowerment System (EES)**, innovated in the mid-1990s. It has been tested and applied to businesses for over 20 years. This methodology is called BEES because it is aimed toward the creation and development of Black community economic empowerment. The word Black (African-American) gives EES a focal point to help improve its proficiency in attaining the goals and objectives of BEES. Historically, from the times of Emancipation, Reconstruction, the Jim Crow Era, the Civil Rights Era, and now this "Post-Racial" Era, the sustainable and economic rise of African-Americans has been at best unavailable for the masses. There have been systems in place to block or hinder our progress, and it appears in our current polarized political climate, that now more than ever, is the time to create and generate systems that work for us. **The Black Economic Empowerment System (BEES)** could be the very system that puts the economic failures of the African-American community in the past—forever.

The BEES uses the Profit Consulting Methodology (PCM) as its foundation. Therefore, the genesis of the Black Economic Empowerment System is the Profit Consulting Methodology. The Profit Consulting Methodology can apply four (4) dimensions and six analyses to successfully complete any of its projects. Once the goals and objectives are specified on a PCM project, their associated resources and activities are determined; that data is then formatted, displayed, and channeled toward the goals and objectives to help secure the success of the project.

PCM can be applied to any type of project in any field or industry. Thus, combining PCM with BEES gives the Profit Consulting Methodology a systematic approach and the laser focus needed to successfully create and develop Black community economic empowerment projects. The combination of PCM and BEES first came to fruition following the Million Man March.

The BEES not only applies elements of PCM, but also has its own internal parts, and those 6 Primary Parts are called:

Community Business Organization (CBO)

Associated Community Participants (ACP)
Associated Vendors (AV)
Associated Suppliers (AS)
Community Investors (CI)
Community Corporation (CC)

A Community Business Organization (CBO) is an entity that advocates for the community (ACP).

Associated Community Participants (ACP) are people who have an agreement with their CBO.

Associated Vendors (AV) are sellers of goods and/or services.

Associated Suppliers (AS) are merchants who sell goods and/or services to Associated Vendors.

Community Investors (CI) are people or business entities who also have an agreement with their CBO.

A Community Corporation (CC) is the entity that will execute the operational and financial structure of its associated BEES project.

These six parts are intricate components of any Black community economic empowerment project's success. They are all applied systematically, and this system will be detailed further in Phase Two.

PHASE TWO

"A group's ability to compete is determined by its internal cohesiveness and self-interest."

Dr. Claud Anderson

THE THEORY and APPROACH of the BEES

Welcome to the theory and approach of the Black Economic Empowerment System.

As I stated in the beginning and will repeat here, I learned that the Profit Consulting Methodology's ultimate power is to teach you how to clearly define your goal and look at that goal as a project.

This theory has been absolutely proven over and over again. Because of this, I am passionate about bringing this to my community in a way that is feasible, digestible, and accessible to all who are willing to learn, apply, and make a sustaining, economic, and empowering difference.

It has been my experience that when this approach is applied correctly, it will ensure your success on any project.

Let's look at this another way. Nature gives us the proof of this theory and approach metaphorically in **how honeybees live and work.** The parallels are uncanny—down to the acronym of the title of this book—which is why we used it to draw the parallel and create the logo. The formation of a colony of hives is not unlike the formation of these community projects. Let's look at the way beehives are created.

Honeybees live in a beehive, just as we would live in a community. The beehive consists of one queen bee, male drones, and the female worker bees, nurse female bees, the hive, larvae, and of course honey. Honeybees live within these hives for one purpose only. Their sole mission is to produce and reproduce, or in other words, colonize and recolonize by cross-pollinating flowers and trees to produce beeswax for shelter (honeycomb) and honey for food. This cyclical process is a perfect analogy to use in exploring and understanding the BEES theory.

The queen bee's single purpose is to lay eggs (reproduce). However, for the sake of this analogy, we will feed the myth and say the queen is also holding court— serving as the resource for making the rules of the operation of the hive. Let's liken the queen bee's role to that of the CBO (the goal of the CBO is to reproduce and profit from its product and be a stable resource and asset to the community).

The worker bee's job is to scout for nectar and pollen to create a wealth of honey and beeswax for personal fulfillment and for the hive (community). Here, we'll ascribe to the worker bees the role of the ACPs.

The drone bee serves only to mate and fertilize the queen bee repeatedly, because she can produce nearly 1,500 eggs per day for the hive. Here, we can say the the drone is like the AV, as the AV supplies the ACPs.

The nurse bee's (the young worker bees not ready to leave the nest) role is to produce and supply the larvae with bee milk or royal jelly. The nurse bee is the AS, as the AS distributes to increase the size of the community.

The larvae's job is to grow fully, nourished by the investment, and provide a return of the investment (ROI) to the hive by multiplying the workforce, and thus the CI.

And last but not least, the honeycomb itself is the hive—the framework for production—allowing every other role to have its place and function intricately woven within the hexagonal (intact and highly functional) structure of the honeycomb; it is, in essence, the CC.

The Six Primary Parts of BEES & Honeybees

Community Business Org (CBO)	Queen bee
Associated Community Participant (ACP)	Worker bees
Associated Vendors (AV)	Drone bees
Associated Suppliers (AS)	Nurse bees
Community Investors (CI)	Larvae
Community Corporation (CC)	Hive

This analogy is very close in functions and provides a universal and memorable visual to demonstrate the purpose of the roles and the critically cyclical nature within the Black Economic Empowerment System.

Theoretically, if all primary parts of the BEES operate and perform like nature's honeybees, then the BEES communities can produce and reproduce and colonize and recolonize and swarm their way to and from one successful and sustainable hive/CBO to another, and another, and so on. Success breeds success.

This core foundation enables BEES to meet and exceed community goals and objectives.

Billionaire businessman, Richard Branson states, *"Starting your own business isn't a job–it's a way of life."*

The BEES is not only a business system, it's a way of life.

SO LET'S TAKE A LOOK AT THESE 3 EXAMPLES OF BEES AND ITS FOUNDATION IN ACTION BELOW.

<u>Example 1</u>:
ACTIVITY BASED COSTING

My first Activity Based Costing project. My client wanted to find out how much it cost to manufacture a specific motor part. Even though I had never stepped foot in a manufacturing plant I knew that 90% of the knowledge and expertise needed to attain my client's goal already existed within the plant. By combining the ABC methodology with the knowledge and expertise that already existed within the plant I knew I could assist my client in attaining their goal. Over time I learned to systemize the approach I used on my first ABC project, and that four step approach was as follows:

1. Think of the desired goal as a project, a project that requires certain activities (units of work) and resources (things that are consumed, and/or things that are generated) to take place in order to reach the goal that has been set;

2. Gather information/intelligence about the activities and resources that are associated with the goal from personnel that are knowledgeable;

3. Format and display the information/intelligence gathered about the associated activities and resources, and lastly;

4. Channel that formatted and displayed information/intelligence toward the desired goal.

The way I applied the four steps above on my first ABC project was by determining the goal and the activities and resources associated with that goal. Then I went to the plant and gathered information/intelligence about the associated activities and resources from employees that had been there for many years. They already knew roughly how much it cost to manufacture the motor part that the project was about. Plus, they knew different ways the cost of manufacturing that part could be reduced. However, their knowledge was fragmented (meaning one person knew one portion about cost savings and another person knew another portion), and they did not have a sufficient way to quantify what they knew. As a result, that knowledge base was constrained.

I applied the ABC methodology to gather, format, display (displaying allows everyone to see the same picture, which empowers a project to achieve its desired result) and channel the data towards the goal. In other words, I applied the knowledge base that already existed in the plant to calculate and symbolically display the cost of the motor part. Once that cost was calculated and displayed with an explanation, it empowered my client to reduce the cost of manufacturing the motor part because the display visually highlighted some inefficiencies for all to see.

Hence, the visual displays were the channels used to attain the goal.

Example 2:
PROFIT CONSULTING METHODOLOGY:

For example on my first Profit Consulting Methodology project my client, an insurance broker, wanted to increase the profitability of their many distinct insurance lines of business. Once again, even though I had no insurance experience, I knew that 90% of the knowledge and expertise needed to attain my client's goal already existed within the company. So by combining the Profit Consulting Methodology with the knowledge and expertise that already existed within the insurance company I knew I could assist my client in attaining their goal by applying a four-step approach:

__Step 1.__ Think of the desired goal as a project, a project that requires certain activities (units of work) and resources (things that are consumed, and/or things *that are generated) to take place in order to reach the goal that has been set;*

Step 2. Gather information /intelligence about the activities and resources from knowledgeable personnel;

Step 3. Format and display the information/intelligence gathered about the associate activities and resources; and

Step 4. Channel that formatted and displayed information/intelligence toward the desired goal.

The way I applied the four steps above on my insurance client's PCM project was by determining the activities and resources that were associated with the goal. Then I went to the personnel involved with each line of insurance to gather information/intelligence about the associated activities and resources. However, the knowledge was fragmented because the personnel only focused on their specific line of business. Hence, impeding the cohesiveness needed to attain the desired goal. At least until I applied PCM to gather, format, display (displaying allows everyone to see the same picture, which empowers a project to achieve its desired result) and channel the data towards the goal. In other words, I consolidated the knowledge base that already existed from each line to increase the overall profitability of my client's business. Once I symbolically displayed the information/intelligence I gathered for all to see, it empowered my client. The display highlighted that my client was allocating extra financing to each line of business based on the percentage of overall expense each particular line represented. For example, if Insurance Line A represented 60% of the company's overall expense, then Insurance Line A would receive 60% of the allocated financing. Hence, this method stimulated insurance line managers to increase their expenses to receive a larger portion of the corporate financial allocation. However, once this was displayed for all to see, it was concluded that this method was not good for the overall company. My client discovered that if the financing was allocated based on the percentage of profit each particular line represented, instead of their percentage of expense, the insurance line managers would focus on increasing their profitability, instead of their expense. As a result of this change in methods the profitability of each distinct insurance line of business increased, resulting in my client's goal being attained.

Example 3:
PCM and BEES

For example on my first Black Economic Empowerment System project my client was a community organization. One of their primary goals was to economically empower their community by creating jobs, businesses, attracting investors and generating wealth. I knew after hearing their goals that by applying the Profit Consulting Methodology (PCM) and the Black Economic Empowerment System (BEES) this project could be successfully completed. On a Black Economic Empowerment System project there are four phases to success and they are:

1. Let your client determine their goals;

2. *Educate all relevant parties how BEES works and how its components can be applied toward their goals;*

3. *Let the relevant parties determine alternate approaches to attain their goals, and then select the best approach, lastly;*

4. *Implement a method that applies the selected approach to attain their goals.*

The way I progressed through the 4 phases on my first BEES project was to let my client determine their own goals, and then I had multiple meeting to educate them on how BEES works and how its components can be applied toward their goals. This education helped them devise alternative approaches, within the Black Economic Empowerment System's scope. And since the alternative approaches were all within the scope of BEES, it made it easier to determine the best approach. We determined on this project, to find a community vendor that would give back to the community in exchange for a market (an increase in sales). It was determined that the vendors would need to sell goods that a wide range of community participants would have interest in, and that the pricing for those goods should range from low to high. By clearly defining the best approach it made finding the target that much easier. Thus, we found a community vendor that met all the specifications. In addition, the community vendor agreed, in exchange for the designated market, he would give 20% of each sale back to the community. As matter of fact, the day he verbally agreed to become a part of BEES he had multiple sales that same day. The implementation of BEES with my client's first vendor created a blueprint for duplicating the process with multiple community vendors (large, small, new, etc.), which will greatly assist them with attaining their goals.

NOW HERE'S ONE MORE LOOK at the SIX PRIMARY PARTS of the BEES and THEIR FULL DEFINITIONS.

Part 1 - COMMUNITY BUSINESS ORGANIZATION (CBO)

A Community Business Organization is an entity that functions as an advocate for the community. It is a place where all the agreements, policies, and procedures (rules) are established for participating and operating within its BEES project. This will include creating criteria and providing direction to help insure the success of Associated Vendors, Associated Suppliers, and the overall project.

Part 2 - ASSOCIATED COMMUNITY PARTICIPANT (ACP)

An Associated Community Participant is a person who has an agreement with his/her CBO, which states the Associated Community Participant will patronize Associated Vendor(s) in exchange for the creation of wealth and resources within the community—including personal financial gain.

Part 3 - ASSOCIATED VENDOR (AV)

An Associated Vendor is a person or business who sells directly to the ACP. In addition, all AVs will have an agreement with their CBO. It states that in exchange for any increase in profit margin resulting from ACP patronage, the AVs will retain a previously agreed upon amount of that increase and distribute a previously agreed upon amount to its associated Community Corporation.

Part 4 - ASSOCIATED SUPPLIER (AS)

An Associated Supplier is a person or a business who sells to AVs. In addition, each AS will have an agreement with its associated CBO, which states that in exchange for any increase in profit margin that results from AV sales, the AS will retain an agreed-upon amount of that increase and distribute the to its associated CC.

Part 5 - COMMUNITY INVESTOR (CI)

A Community Investor is a person or a business who invests financial and/or non-financial resources in its associated Community Corporation in exchange for a return on investment (ROI). More specifically within BEES, a CI is a person or a business who invests resources (which is a productive factor, such as money, labor, land, energy, material, etc., required to accomplish a desired outcome) in exchange for a financial or non-financial reward. Additionally, all CIs will have an agreement with their CBO. It states how the investment and ROI will be applied within BEES.

Part 6 - COMMUNITY CORPORATION (CC)

A Community Corporation is the entity that will execute the operational and financial structure of its associated BEES project. It will make sure the community goals and objectives that have been set forth are: implemented, executed, and continuously improved.

PHASE THREE

"Progress is the attraction that moves humanity."

Marcus Garvey

THE APPLICATION of the BEES

Welcome to the Application of the BEES. The mission here is to teach you how to assemble and perpetually improve a Black Economic Empowerment System. This phase is divided into three sections:

SECTION 1
The Composition of BEES
SECTION 2
How to Assemble/Create BEES
SECTION 3
How to Continuously Improve BEES

SECTION 1
The Composition of BEES

The Components Within Each Primary Part of BEES

The six Primary Parts have been defined previously. We will now review each part in a deeper dive to understand their associated components in greater detail.

Part 1 of BEES:
THE COMMUNITY BUSINESS
ORGANIZATION (CBO)

As we learned earlier, (and I am repeating here for better retention of the concepts) CBO is an entity that acts as an advocate for its Associated Community Participants. It is the place where all the agreements, policies, and procedures (rules) are established for operating within a BEES' project. It is also the CBO's responsibility to insure that BEES' four primary objectives are implemented, and those objectives are to:

1. Empower at the community level first, and then find common denominators with other communities (BEES' projects) to expand the empowerment on a larger scale.

2. Let the community/ACP help define what economic empowerment means to them and the goals associated with it.

3. Insure that the community's BEES allows for resources to be entered, wealth to be generated, a percentage of that wealth to be invested into the community, and a percentage to be distributed back to the ACP.

4. Insure that the community's BEES is totally transparent and easy to comprehend.

NOTE: This bottom-up collaborative approach with transparency is key to establishing trust and full participation. If everyone understands the components and functions of the organization, and is in consensus, it removes the opportunity for ambiguity and creates levels of trust and participation that make the organization successful.

The CBO COMPONENTS are:
I)   The Associated Community Participants (Paying Members)
II)   The Associated Community Participants (Non-Paying Members, if applicable)
III) The Administrative Member(s)
IV)   The Executive Member(s)

Part 2 of BEES:
ASSOCIATED COMMUNITY PARTICIPANTS (ACP)

Associated Community Participants are people who have an agreement with their applicable CBO. It states that they will help increase the Associated Vendor's profit margin by patronizing the Associated

Vendor's business in exchange for rewards (both monetary and non-monetary).

The ACP COMPONENTS are:
I)   Community Residents

II)   Area Residents

III)   Virtual Residents

Part 3 of BEES:
ASSOCIATED VENDOR (AV)

An Associated Vendor is a person or business who sells directly to ACP. In addition, an AV has an agreement with its CBO. It states that in exchange for a profit margin in excess of its original (historical) profit margin, that results from ACP patronage, the AV will retain 100% of the original profit margin: however, the margin in excess of its original profit margin will be divided between the AV and the

Community Corporation based on a predetermined percentage.

The AV COMPONENTS are:

I)   ACP Patrons

II)   Products and/or Services

III)   A Tracking System

Part 4 of BEES:
ASSOCIATED SUPPLIER (AS)

An Associated Supplier is a person or business who sells directly to Associated Vendors. In addition, an AS has an agreement with its CBO, which states that in exchange for a profit margin in excess of its (historical) profit margin, that results from AV purchases, the AS will retain 100% of the original profit margin: however, the margin in excess of its original profit margin will be divided between the AS and the Community Corporation based on a predetermined percentage.

The COMPONENTS of AS are:
I)   AV BUYERS

II)   Goods and/or Services

III)   A Tracking System

Part 5 of BEES:
COMMUNITY INVESTOR (CI)

A Community Investor is a person or a business entity that has an agreement with its applicable CBO. It states that in exchange for investing finances and/or other resources the Community Investor will receive a predetermined return on investment.

The CI COMPONENTS are:
I)   A Personal Investor

II)   A Business Investor

Part 6 of BEES:
Community Corporation (CC)

A Community Corporation is an entity that executes the financial and operational structure of its associated community's BEES. The CC will accomplish this execution by performing six distinct functions/analyses as needed. For smaller BEES projects, the six distinct functions/analyses can be managed by one or a few certified BEES expert(s). For larger BEES projects the six distinct functions or analyses should be departmentalized.

The CC COMPONENTS are:
I)   Activity & Process Flow Analysis
II)   Feasibility & Optimization Analysis
III)   Sensitivity Analysis

IV)   Custom Focus Analysis

V)   Performance Measure Analysis

VI)   Continuous Improvement Analysis

(I)The purpose of the **Activity and Process Flow Analysis** as a function or a department is to determine what the community's BEES is **supposed** to accomplish theoretically based on the community's goals.

(II)The purpose of the **Feasibility and Optimization Analysis** as a function or a department is to determine what the community's BEES is **actually** accomplishing based on the community's goals.

(III)The purpose of the **Sensitivity Analysis** as a function or a department is to determine how a potential change in approach will impact its associated community's BEES based on the community's goals.

(IV) The purpose of the **Customer Focus Analysis** as a function or a department is to determine how well the intra-relationships of the community's BEES are working based on the community's goals.

(V) The purpose of the **Performance Measure Analysis** as a function or a department is to measure the performance of all relevant activities and resources within the community's BEES based on the community's goals.

(VI) The purposes of the **Continuous Improvement Analysis** as a function or a department are to:
   1. Generate specifications/standards that will help create and/or develop the community's BEES.

2. Create stimulants to perpetually improve the community's BEES.

3. Implement indicators that will highlight any deviations from the standards that have been put in place based on the community's goals.

SECTION 2
How to Assemble/Create BEES

A Step-by-Step Approach

Now that you know: (1) the six individual parts of BEES, (2) how those six parts individually operate/function and (3) the components that exist within each of those parts, we are now ready to discuss the step-by-step approach needed to assemble/create BEES. In other words, let's discuss how to bring those six parts together in order to form a Black Economic Empowerment System.

Step 1:
A. Establish a CBO, if one does not already exist.

B. The CBO must establish executive and administrative members.

C. Define the roles and responsibilities of the executive and administrative members, and make sure those roles and responsibilities are aligned with BEES four primary applications.

The 4 Applications of BEES are:

Application I

Make sure the size (area) of the local community is not too large; if it is there could be a vast difference in goals and objectives, which could break down the cohesiveness needed to empower a BEES project. If, therefore, the community size (area) becomes an issue, form as many (multiple) CBOs as needed. Once multiple CBOs are established, they can find common denominators that exist between them, and the duplication of this approach can then be used to indirectly expand the empowerment.

Application II

Let the community define the goals of BEES and define what empowerment means to them. This will lead to a greater understanding and support base of a BEES' project.

Application III

Make sure the rewards and benefits of BEES are fair and cyclical; what a person or entity contributes to a project should be returned proportionally. In addition, make sure the **project is profitable**. This is known as BEES **Financial Principle**.

Application IV

Make sure all relevant aspects (both financial and non-financial) of a BEES' project are totally transparent. **This will insure that all things are done righteously,** which is known as BEES' **Moral Principle**.

Once BEES' Financial Principle and Moral Principle are implemented correctly the foundation of **the project will "feel**

right," which is known as BEES' **Spiritual Principle**.

Step 2: The CBO should have its initial meeting with a Certified BEES Expert to provide a general overview and definition of BEES—plus the mission/goals/objectives of BEES (based on preliminary information received from the community).

Step 3: The CBO Executive(s)/Certified BEES Expert should create the CBO's agreements, policies, and procedures (rules) for the Associated Community Participants.

Step 4: At the end of the second meeting membership classification (ACP Paying Member and ACP Non-Paying Member) should be determined.

Step 5: The CBO executive(s) should hold its first meeting with potential Associated Vendors where a Certified BEES Expert can provide a general overview and definition of BEES—plus its mission/goals/objectives.

Step 6: The CBO executive(s)/Certified BEES Expert should take into account the data it received from the first AV meeting and use that data to create the CBO's agreements, policies, and procedures (rules) for the Associate Vendor(s).

Step 7: At the end of the second meeting, (Associated Vendors) membership classification should be determined; determine who will be classified as an Associated Vendor, who will be classified as a potential Associated Vendor, and who will be classified as N/A (Not Applicable).

Step 8: The CBO's executives should hold its first meeting with potential Associated Suppliers (at the appropriate time) where a Certified BEES Expert can provide a general overview and definition of BEES—plus its mission/goals/objectives.

Step 9: The CBO's executive(s)/Certified BEES Expert should take into account the data it received from the first (AS) meeting and use that data to create the CBO's agreements, policies, and procedures (rules) for the Associated Supplier(s).

Step 10: At the end of the second meeting (Associated Suppliers) membership classification should be determined; determine who will be classified as an Associated Supplier, who will be classified as a potential Associated Supplier, and who will be classified as N/A (Not Applicable).

Step 11(a): The CBO's Certified BEES Expert(s) must help establish the Community Corporation, which will involve voting in the CC's Executives and Administrators, and defining their roles and responsibilities.

Step 11(b): The CC's Certified BEES Expert(s) must determine: (1) if the six analyses will be performed by an individual(s) or as departments, and (2) how the six analytical functions or departments will operate.

Step 11(c): The CC's executive(s) /Certified BEES Expert(s) must determine how information will flow within the entity.

Step 11(d): The CC's executive(s) /Certified BEES Expert(s) must insure that a transparent system is implemented which exposes: (1) all relevant roles and responsibilities to establish accountability, and (2) all pertinent data (both financial and non-financial).

Step 11(e): The CC's executive(s) /Certified BEES Expert(s) must determine what financing and resources are needed and desired. Once that is known they can set up a meeting with potential Community Investors to help attain those goals.

Step 12: The goals of the first meeting with potential Community Investors are to:

> A. Discuss what the community needs in terms of financial and non-financial resources.
> B. Discuss what the potential CI can provide to the community in terms of financial and non-financial resources.
> C. Discuss the potential Community

Investor's return on investment.

D. Discuss the transparency of the Community's BEES, and how and when The CI can get access to all financial and non-financial data.

Step 13: After the CC's executive(s) /Certified BEES Expert(s) first meeting with potential Community Investor(s), an agreement(s) must be created (and eventually signed) for potential Community Investor(s) to actually become Community Investor(s).

Special Note(s): The CI agreement should be based on the discussion that took place between the CC representatives(s) and the potential Community Investor(s).

Step 14: A second meeting should take place between the CC representative(s)and the potential Community Investor(s) with the objective of having both parties sign the created agreement. Once the agreement is signed the potential CI will be classified as a CI.

S E C T I O N 3
How to Continuously Improve BEES

You Must Have <u>GENERATORS,</u> <u>STIMULATORS,</u> and <u>INDICATORS</u> throughout BEES

They are the engines for perpetual improvement.

Now that you have learned the parts and components of BEES, and how to put the parts and components of BEES in place and in order, you are now ready to learn how to move that assembled/created BEES in a way that perpetually gets better. In other words, you are now ready to learn **How to Continuously Improve BEES.**

To continuously improve BEES, you must have **Generators, Simulators**, and

Indicators (GSI) in their proper places. However, before we talk about where GSIs should be located, let's define what they are.

THE DEFINITIONS OF GSI WITHIN BEES

Generators are benchmarks, or standards, or performance measures, or specifications, that are created to help insure the goals and objectives of BEES are being met.

Stimulators are incentives, or bait, or motivators, or enticements that are put in place after Generators have been created to help insure the goals and objectives of BEES are not only being met, but also continuously improved.

Indicators are notifications, or alerts, or disclosures, or expositions that are put in place after Generators have been created to help insure any deviated action, or movement from the goals and objectives of BEES are displayed.

THE LOCATIONS OF
GSI WITHIN BEES

When it comes to GSI, one of the first things to **REMEMBER** is all three must exist in the same places. In other words, if you create a Generator for something, it must have a Stimulator, along with an Indicator assigned to it also. GSIs should be assigned to all relevant activities and resources that relate to BEES' goals and objectives. And, GSI data should be accessible to all.

REVENUE DRIVER | WEALTHDRIVER | INVESTMENT CONTRIBUTION CREATES BOUNCE WITHIN BEES

The reason you see Revenue Driver and then the words Wealth Driver next to it is because within BEES, a Revenue Driver leads to the creation of wealth. Also, before we move on, it is important to remember that within BEES, a Revenue Driver is called a Wealth Driver or an Investment Contribution (IC). With that being said, let's talk about how an Investment Contribution leads to the creation of Wealth.

Each IC is considered a Bounce. A Bounce happens when money is spent and/or invested in a BEES' community, and a portion of that money is retained by the community.

Therefore, more Bounces within a BEES' community leads to more money and resources, and more money and resources leads to the **CREATION OF WEALTH.**

NOW LET'S REVIEW A VISUAL DISPLAY OF HOW BEES FLOW

A GENERAL OVERVIEW OF THE BLACK ECONOMIC EMPOWERMENT SYSTEM (BEES)

NOTES: BEES OVERVIEW DISPLAY

Special Note :
All persons and entities that want to be a part of a specific BEES project can only do so by going through the project's associated Community Business Organization (CBO). A Community Business Organization (CBO) is an entity which functions as an advocate for the Associated Community Participants (ACP). It is a place where all the agreements, policies, and procedures (rules) are established for operating within the BEES. This includes creating criteria to help insure the success of Associated Vendors and Associated Suppliers. In addition, the organization will provide directions to those vendors and suppliers that do not meet the criteria which have been established so that they may return at some later date in a satisfactory capacity. Hence, this the (quasi) LEGISLATIVE BRANCH.

Note 1 - Associated Community Participants (ACP)
are people that have an agreement with its CBO. It states the ACP will patronize Associated Vendors in exchange for the creation of wealth and resources within their community, and also for personal financial gain. In addition, ACP (the community) will be the ultimate judges of how successful their BEES is, hence this is the (quasi) JUDICIAL BRANCH.

Note 2 - Associated Vendor (AV)
is a person or business that sells directly to the ACP. In addition, all AV's will have an agreement with its CBO. It states that in exchange for any increase in profit margin that results from ACP patronage, the AV will retain an agreed upon amount of that increase to its associated Community Corporation.

Note 3 - Associated Supplier (AS)
is a person or business that sells to Associated Vendors. In addition, all Associated Suppliers will have an agreement with its CBO. It states that results from AV sales, the AS will retain an agreed upon an amount of that increase and distribute an agreed upon amount of that increase to its associated Community Corporation.

Note 4 - Community Investor (CI)
is a person or business that invests resources in its associated Community Corporation in exchange for return on the investment (ROI). More specifically within BEES needs a person or business that invests resources in exchange for financial or nonfinancial reward. In addition, all Community Investors will have an agreement with its CBO which states how the ROI will be applied within BEES.

Note 5 - Community Corporation (CC)
is the entity that will execute the operational and the financial structure of its associated BEES project. It will make sure that the community goals that have been set forth are implemented, executed and continuously improved. Therefore, the Community Corporation's role is to insure that all necessary functions and resources needed to attain the community's goal are implemented, executed and continuously improved this is the (quasi) EXECUTIVE BRANCH.

CONCLUSION

You were given the brief history of the PCM, and the evolution of BEES and its overview, to provide you with a better understanding of how each functions. It is our belief that the more you understand their functionalities, the higher your comprehension level of each of their powers and your ability to take advantage of those powers. That is why we offer the two training classes.

Essentially there are two parts to this training system: **PCM** and **BEES**. **Profit**

Consulting Methodology (PCM) Training is a Prerequisite of the Black Economic

The two courses include training for: (1) How to improve the performance, profitability, and/or process flow of any project, and 2) How to create and develop black community economic empowerment projects.

Those two training classes are called, **(1) The Profit Consulting Methodology Online Training Class.** Once you complete the PCM online training class, and pass its test (which you can take as many times as needed to get an 80% or better), you will become a Certified Profit Consulting Expert.

THE PCM Training Components Include:

A. The Core Elements of ABC

B. Financial Dimensions of Costs

C. The Process Flow Dimension of Costs

D. The Financial Dimension of Revenue

E. The Process Flow Dimension of Revenue

F. The Six Analyses of PCM

    a. Activity Based Costing

    b. Activity Based Resource and,

(2) The Black Economic Empowerment System Online Training Class.

Once you complete the BEES online training class, and pass its test (which you can take as many times as needed to get an 80% or better), you will become a Certified Black Economic Empowerment System Expert.

The BEES Training Components Include:

A. A detailed explanation of the general overview of this book.

Special Note(s): After you become certified you will have the option to join an online forum (which will be equivalent to becoming a part of a virtual firm) where you can discuss/exchange ideas about past, present, or future projects with other certified experts. So you will never have to take on a project alone.

However, to become a Certified Black Economic Empowerment System Expert you must already be a Certified Profit Consulting Expert. In other words, PCM training is a prerequisite of BEES training because the Profit Consulting Methodology is the foundation of the Black Economic Empowerment System.

It is our objective to insure that those people, who want more detail and the opportunity to develop and become a distinguished expert of the Profit Consulting Methodology and the Black Economic Empowerment System, can do so. And it is our belief that our online training classes will help facilitate those opportunities.

To receive training online as a Certified Profit Consulting Expert all you have to do is go to the **www.armara-training.com** website, and select the Get Certified button, which is located in the right upper hand corner of its homepage.

To receive training online to become a Certified Black Economic Empowerment System Expert, go to the: **www.economicempowermentservices.com** website, and select the Get Certified button, which is located in the right upper hand corner of its homepage.

In addition, to follow us and learn about our upcoming events, and other exciting news, please visit us at:

**www.Facebook.com/
Economic Empowerment Services, Inc.**

www.Twitter.com@EesARice

AFTERWORD

Not since the 1920s and 1930s has there been a time when African-Americans "freely" grouped and formed thriving and prosperous communities that were created and wholly supported by and for them. A by-product of racial-segregation no doubt, being just one generation post Reconstruction, but also out of necessity to survive in the racially tense environments. We had vibrant townships where the money circulated within the community multiple times before it went outside: Harlem, NY, Rosewood, FL, the Fillmore District in San Francisco, CA, Allensworth, CA, and one of the most famously known, "Black Wall Street" in the district of Greenwood in Tulsa, OK. Black Wall Street was a proven and prime example of BEES before it was bombed. One May 31, 1921, over 300 African-Americans were massacred in a three-day killing spree (misnamed a 'race riot'). Actually, it was an outright terrorist attack where no one was ever charged or punished for this heinous crime against humanity. To add insult to injury, over 6,000 black residents were arrested and detained for defending their homes and businesses and trying to stay alive.

Dr. Claud Anderson, author of many books on socio-economics and race including, *Powernomics, The Intersection of Race and Economics*, states it this way, *"We spend approximately 97-98% of our all our money outside of our own community... what that does is, it makes the other groups enriched. They now are living off of two incomes. They live on 100% of their money and on 98% of our money. And what are we left with, is two percent... "*

Think about that, just two percent (2%) is left to produce wealth—a virtual impossibility.

The business model and methodology of the **BEES** is one that provides something for everyone, starting in micro-communities (right where you are) that build upon the activities within those communities and then expands outward to colonize and recolonize. You can start **right where you are**, with the people and resources immediately available and within reach. The Black Economic Empowerment System is a blueprint and this century's new movement to black community wealth generation and sustainability. The buzz is growing, and the **BEES** is available for you.

We are embarking on a new intellectual and economic evolution. Learn the system and join the swarm!

ABOUT THE AUTHOR

Business Leader and Author, **Anthony Rice, Jr.,** has been an entrepreneur for over 22 years and is currently the President of Armara, Inc., a Profit Consulting Methodology firm and President of Economic Empowerment Services, Inc., (EES) and economic empowerment implementation company. His success has been achieved primarily by referrals, which is a powerful way to do and sustain business. Anthony's philosophy is "There is a solution to every problem, concern, and issue; you just have to know how and where to find it." And he is an expert problem solver.

Anthony attended Howard University and Westfield State College and earned a B.S., in Management/Accounting. He is currently serving as the Vice Chairman of the Travelers Aid Society of Metropolitan Detroit, a nonprofit organization, providing support to Detroit's homeless and displaced families.

Anthony works and resides in Southfield, MI, with his family.

To Order Books, or Contact Anthony for Speaking Engagements:

Website:
www.economicempowermentservices.com
Email:
Aricejr1@msn.com | Phone: (313)505-0700

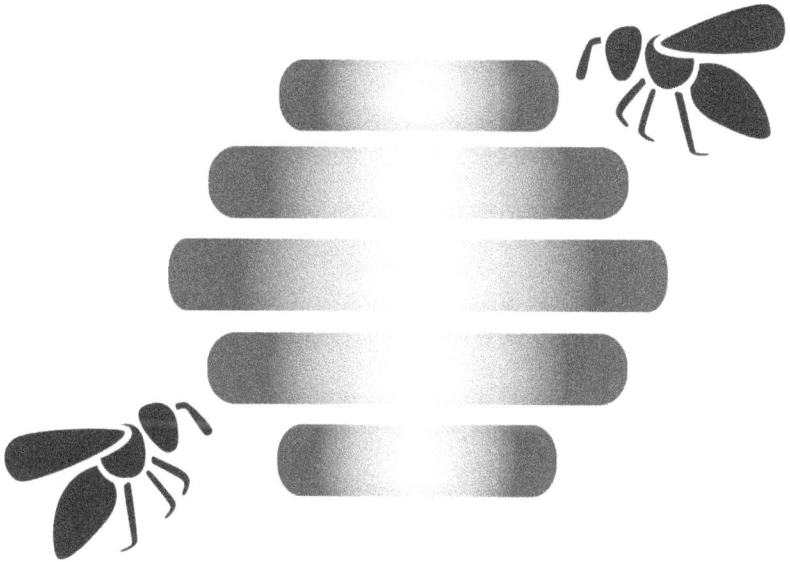

www.ingramcontent.com/pod-product-compliance
Lightning Source LLC
Chambersburg PA
CBHW061836220326
41599CB00027B/5300